Fun with Dolphins

Bobbie Kalman

🌴 Crabtree Publishing Company

www.crabtreebooks.com

Created by Bobbie Kalman

for Lindsey Potter, remembering the fun we had with dolphins

Author and Publisher
Bobbie Kalman

Editorial director
Niki Walker

Editors
Kathryn Smithyman
Amanda Bishop

Art director
Robert MacGregor

Design
Bobbie Kalman
Samantha Crabtree

Production coordinator
Heather Fitzpatrick

Photo research
Samantha Crabtree
Laura Hysert

Consultant
Patricia Loesche, Ph.D.,
Animal Behavior Program,
Department of Psychology,
University of Washington

Special thanks to
Diane Sweeney and Patrick McLain at Dolphin Quest, Samantha Crabtree and Marc Crabtree, Lindsey Potter and Gloria Corea, Loreen Matsushima and Mike Osborne at Sea Life Park Hawaii, and Jake Jaskolski

Photographs
© Phillip Colla/oceanlight.com: cover (Olympic medalist in synchronized swimming, Mikako Kotani appears on cover), pages 6 (Olympic gold medalist in swimming, Matt Biondi, appears on pages 6 and 21), 9 (bottom), 11 (right), 21 (top), 23 (bottom right)
Photos courtesy of Dolphin Quest Hawaii, located at the Kahala Mandarin Oriental Hawaii: back cover, title page, pages 12, 14 (bottom), 15 (top left), 25 (top), 26
Bobbie Kalman: taken at Sea Life Park Hawaii, page 11 (bottom left); taken at Dolphin Quest Hawaii at the Kahala Mandarin Oriental Hawaii; pages 5 (top), 13 (bottom), 15 (top right), 25 (center), 27 (bottom), 31 (top and bottom two); taken at Dolphin Quest Hawaii at the Hilton Waikoloa Village: pages 4, 13 (top right); taken elsewhere, pages 14 (top), 17 (top 3), 22, 23 (top right and bottom left), 30
Photo courtesy of Sea Life Park Hawaii: page 5 (bottom)
© Michael S. Nolan/wildlifeimages.net: pages 20, 21 (bottom)
© James D. Watt/wattstock.com: pages 7 (bottom), 9 (top), 19 (top)
SeaPics/seapics.com: © Jeff Jaskolski: pages 16, 17 (bottom); © Doug Perrine: pages 8, 10 (top), 11 (top left), 15 (bottom)/taken at Dolphin Quest Hawaii at the Hilton Waikoloa Village; © Masa Ushioda: page 7 (top); © Ingrid Visser: page 13 (top left); © Doc White: page 18
© Brandon Cole/brandoncole.com: page 19 (bottom)
Other images by Digital Vision and Digital Stock

Illustrations and artwork:
© Jeff Wilkie/jeffwilkie.com: pages 24, 29 (bottom)
Tiffany Wybouw: borders and decorative dolphins
Barbara Bedell: page 12, 24
Margaret Amy Reiach: back cover, page 21 (girls)
© Robert Thomas: pages 3, 29 (top)

Crabtree Publishing Company

www.crabtreebooks.com   1-800-387-7650

PMB 16A
350 Fifth Avenue
Suite 3308
New York, NY
10118

612 Welland Avenue
St. Catharines
Ontario
Canada
L2M 5V6

73 Lime Walk
Headington
Oxford
OX3 7AD
United Kingdom

Cataloging-in-Publication Data
Kalman, Bobbie
    Fun with dolphins / Bobbie Kalman.
        p. cm. -- (Dolphin worlds)
This book provides information and activities that help readers to experience the life of dolphins.
    ISBN 0-7787-1165-X (RLB) -- ISBN 0-7787-1185-4 (pbk.)
    1. Dolphins--Juvenile literature. [1. Dolphins.] I. Title.
QL737.C432 K3763 2003
599.53--dc21

LC 2002014605

Contents

Everyone loves dolphins!

Why do people love dolphins? We love dolphins because they make us feel good. Although dolphins cannot change their expressions, they always seem to be smiling. We can't help feeling happy when someone smiles at us. People do not just love dolphins for their smiles, though. We love them because they are intelligent, playful, and friendly. They remind us of ourselves. Dolphins also seem to have a sense of humor. Dolphins are fun!

Do dolphins like us?

People want to touch dolphins, play with dolphins, swim with dolphins, and even kiss dolphins. These amazing animals have the power to win our hearts, and we want them to like us, too. No one knows for sure if dolphins really like people, but we do know that they are curious about us. Some even choose to be in our company. Dolphins are social animals that hunt, rest, travel, and play with other dolphins. They might simply see us as another type of playmate—and dolphins love to play!

Many people dream of seeing dolphins up close. Some marine parks offer programs that give people a chance to interact with dolphins. These girls are receiving a lesson in dolphin training. They are giving a dolphin a signal called "station." When it sees this signal, the dolphin knows to pay attention because it will soon receive a command.

Social creatures

There are a few **species** of dolphins that live alone, but most live in groups. Small family groups of dolphins are called **pods**. Large groups of hundreds or even thousands of dolphins are called **schools**. Schools often include more than one species of dolphin. Living in groups helps dolphins survive. They work together to fight off **predators**. Many species of dolphins hunt together. They help one another find **prey** and then cooperate to trap it. Some dolphins spend the whole night hunting in large schools. Others hunt in small groups during the day. After a successful hunt, many dolphins make spectacular leaps out of the water (see opposite page).

Some wild dolphins, such as these Atlantic spotted dolphins, are curious enough to swim near people or boats, but many dolphins avoid people.

Learning through play

Most dolphins raise their young in groups. Groups provide "baby-sitters" and teachers for dolphin calves. Since dolphins are not born with the **instinct** of how to hunt, their mothers and other dolphins in the group teach them. Sometimes they make a game of tossing fish or squid into the air for the calves to catch. After hunting, many dolphins play. They seem to enjoy **bow-riding**, or getting pushed along by the waves in front of a boat, and **wake-riding** in the frothy bubbles behind it.

These dolphins are bow-riding, or catching a free ride in front of a boat.

Dolphin games

Many animals play when they are young, but most stop playing when they are older. Dolphins spend a great deal of their time playing—even as adults. Dolphins in the wild pick up objects they find and use them in their games. They also make their own toys by blowing bubble rings, such as the one shown above. They try to keep the rings from rising to the surface. They also take turns swimming through the bubbles to feel the tingle of the air against their sensitive skin. Mothers often blow bubble rings to tickle their calves.

Pass it on!

Another favorite game played by wild dolphins is similar to tag or catch. Dolphins play it with anything—leaves, seaweed, plastic bags, or other found objects. They carry these objects on their fins, **flukes**, or jaws. Sometimes they drop them and allow other dolphins to catch them. A mother and calf, shown below, often play this gentle version of the game.

Catch it if you can!

Sometimes dolphins chase a dolphin carrying an object and try to snatch it away. An even more exciting version of this game is "Stand Off." A dolphin with an object drops it, and two rows of dolphins line up facing one another, with the object floating between them. When one dolphin gives the "Go!" signal, all the dolphins scramble to try and grab the object.

9

Putting on a show

Scientists are not sure why dolphins leap, spin, and dance, but they have a few ideas. To swim faster, dolphins **porpoise**, or leap out of the water as they swim. By porpoising, dolphins can breathe more easily and avoid the **drag**, or pull of the water against their bodies. Dolphins may leap high out of the water to let other dolphins know where they are or to show them where prey is located. Spinner dolphins might spin as they leap to shake off **remoras**, which are small fish with suckers on their mouths that attach themselves to these dolphins. Sometimes hundreds of spinners put on a spectacular show for people in boats. No one knows if they do it for the applause, but it sure seems that way! Scientists cannot say for certain why dolphins leap, but I have seen them jump and spin and dance, and I believe they are doing it just to have fun!

These dolphins may be leaping to show direction.

These spotted dolphins are porpoising to swim faster.

(top left) A spinner dolphin leaps high out of the ocean and then spins several times before dropping into the water again. (bottom left) Two bottlenose dolphins perform a joyful dance. (above) These Atlantic spotted dolphins seem to be waltzing! A swimmer joins them in their graceful dance.

Dolphin humor

No one knows for sure if dolphins have a sense of humor, but they do play a lot of tricks! Wild dolphins have been known to leap high out of the water and bounce unsuspecting birds off their heads! They also steal fish from some birds. The types of fish they steal are not part of dolphin diets, so the dolphins seem to steal as a prank, rather than as a way of finding food. Dolphins also love to **mimic**, or imitate. They squawk like birds, roar like motorboat engines, and imitate the way people talk, laugh, move, and swim. Sometimes they imitate sharks by arching their backs and pressing their flippers forward—a posture reef sharks take to warn others away from their territories. A favorite dolphin trick is splashing, as shown above and on the right. Sometimes dolphins make a chuckling sound after they have soaked someone.

What are they up to now?
Do these dolphins look a bit mischievous to you? They do to me!

"Fooled you!"
The children snorkeling in this picture were told that they could see these dolphins underwater. As soon as they had their faces down, the dolphins surfaced well ahead of them, chuckling at the joke. Rumor has it that the children are still looking for the dolphins!

"Pay attention to me!"
I spent hundreds of hours visiting a group of dolphins in Hawaii, so some of the dolphins knew me well. One day, as I was sitting on a bench doing some writing, a dolphin that was playing with her ball nearby smashed it down on the water and splashed me, as if to say, "Pay attention to me!"

"Take my picture, already!"
Dolphins seem fascinated by cameras—the bigger, the better. They watch people take pictures of them and have learned the art of posing. As I was about to take pictures of my favorite dolphin one day, she stopped playing with her ball, held it under her chin with her flippers, grinned, and waited patiently for me to take her picture.

Dolphin interactions

Meeting dolphins can happen in a number of ways. Some people take boat trips to see wild dolphins and sometimes swim with them. Some resort hotels on beaches run "swim with dolphins" programs. Dolphin research centers also offer dolphin-interaction opportunities as well as week- or month-long dolphin-training programs. There are even dolphin camps that children can attend! Most people, however, see dolphins at marine parks. Some of these places are better than others. Good dolphin parks make sure that dolphins are treated well, and they educate people about the lives of dolphins in the wild.

By seeing dolphins up close, the children in these photographs learn fascinating facts about dolphins that they will never forget!

(opposite bottom) A dolphin's skin feels smooth and slippery. (above left) Even its tongue feels like silk!
(above right) A dolphin's flipper bones resemble our finger bones. You can see them through the dolphin's skin.
(below) Being in the water with a bottlenose makes you realize just how big these dolphins actually are!

Dolphin camp

Dolphins come into shallow water to interact with the campers. It is fun to see them underwater in their ocean world. They are as curious about this boy as he is about them.

On an island called Roatan, there is a dolphin camp for children from ages five to fourteen. Roatan is an island off the coast of Honduras, a country located in Central America. At the camp, children learn about dolphins and are given several opportunities to interact with them. Children don't just swim with dolphins, however. They also go on nature walks, learn about marine life in oceanside discussions, attend classroom sessions, and go on snorkeling trips. These activities are designed to give children an appreciation of dolphins and of nature.

16

An anatomy lesson

Before the campers meet the dolphins, they need to know a bit about them. In a short classroom session, they start by learning dolphin **anatomy**, or the physical structure of a dolphin's body. They learn how, over millions of years, dolphin ancestors changed from land animals to sea creatures. The children then look at a real dolphin's body and examine the dolphin's flukes, fins, and blowhole.

Meeting the dolphins

When the dolphins come close, it is hard not to hug them. They are gentle and love to have their stomachs scratched, so they swim upside down near the campers. Some of the dolphins open their mouths so the campers can see their teeth and tongues. Others bump the children to get their attention and mimic the way the children move. They seem to be playing a game! How could any camper forget such a wonderful experience?

Learning to snorkel

You need to know how to snorkel if you want to see dolphins underwater. To have a good snorkeling experience, your mask should fit tightly and not allow water to seep in. The end of your snorkel should stick up above water so that you can breathe. Your fins should fit your feet and not come off while you are swimming. Now you are ready to go!

Meeting wild dolphins

The children at the dolphin camp were swimming with trained dolphins, but meeting wild dolphins is another story! In many places, it is now against the law to go within 50 feet (15 m) of wild dolphins. Dolphins don't always follow this law, however. They often approach snorkelers in the ocean. For this reason, people who swim in the ocean should be aware of the **protocol**, or correct behavior, around wild dolphins. The lives of dolphins—and people—may depend on it. Below are some guidelines to follow if you should meet a wild dolphin.

People may think that feeding wild dolphins helps the animals, but it may put their lives in danger.

Dolphin protocol

When meeting wild dolphins, the first and most important rule is: **never feed them**! It is illegal, and it is dangerous to dolphins! Some people feed dolphins foods that make them sick, such as spoiled fish and hot dogs. Feeding dolphins not only makes them sick, but it can also change them from hunters to beggars. Losing their fear of humans can cause dolphins to take risks such as coming too close to boats, where they may be injured by boat propellers. Another important rule is: **never chase dolphins**—either in a boat or in the water. If you see a wild dolphin, **do not swim toward it** or **reach out your hand**.

A dolphin may interpret these actions as aggressive behavior. Wild dolphins rarely tolerate physical contact from humans, so **never try to grab or touch them**. They can be unpredictable—sometimes they are sociable, and sometimes they are not. Mothers feeding their babies will not want you near them, and resting dolphins do not want to be disturbed. Some dolphins are huge animals that can play in aggressive ways. They may hurt people without meaning to. **Never try to hitch a ride on a wild dolphin's back! Move as quietly as you can near wild dolphins**. If they become playful and nip at you, don't panic. Keep your arms at your side and swim away.

Enough is enough!

When dolphins have had enough of people, they will leave. If people follow them, the dolphins may feel threatened. Dolphins that want to be left alone give warning signals. When a dolphin wants someone to back off, it might slap its tail on the water's surface or wag its tail quickly underwater. Another warning signal given by a dolphin is jaw-clapping. This warning shows that a dolphin feels agitated. If a dolphin **charges**, or swims fast toward you, it is definitely time for you to leave. Start moving away immediately. Dolphins rarely hurt people, but it is important to pay attention to their warning signals. Remember that you are in their home!

*When you see a dolphin with its mouth wide open, it is not being friendly. It is **gaping** to show that it feels threatened.*

19

Friendly spotted dolphins

There is a place in the Bahamas, many miles from the nearest land, that is home to a population of 50 to 100 friendly Atlantic spotted dolphins. The place is called Little Bahama Bank, and it is not easy to find! The wild dolphins that live there seem to enjoy the company of humans. Sometimes they play with snorkelers for hours at a time. They swim underneath, beside, and above them, twisting, turning, and even dancing with them (see also pages 6 and 11). The dolphins are so accepting of people, that they nurse their babies in front of them.

The people who swim with these dolphins are mindful of proper **etiquette**, or manners, around dolphins. They wait for the dolphins to come to them and do not try to touch them. Sometimes the dolphins come so close that they look people in the eyes and touch them with their fins. The **juveniles**, or young dolphins, seem to enjoy playing games with the snorkelers. You can tell which dolphins are juveniles by their patterning. They have far fewer spots than adult spotted dolphins have. As they grow older, they will become more spotted.

The dolphin kick

Dolphins are more comfortable with people who use the dolphin kick and do not splash too much when they are swimming. Awkward swimmers can easily startle dolphins with their jerky movements. To learn to swim like a dolphin, you need to keep your knees and ankles together, as if they were a fused dolphin tail. Try to move your body in the way a dolphin does (see below).

(opposite) These curious spotted dolphins surround a snorkeler. One is making eye contact with her.
(top and above) Dolphins feel more comfortable with people who use the dolphin kick. Do you know how to do it?

A snorkeling adventure

Early one morning in Hawaii, a group of us went on a sea kayaking trip. Equipped with snorkels and fins, we were ready to explore a **coral reef**. We had heard that dolphins sometimes entered the bay where we were planning to snorkel, but our guide told us that they didn't always follow the same schedule, so we didn't expect to see them. As we paddled in the direction of the reef, we heard splashing noises. About a hundred spinner dolphins were swimming alongside our kayaks (shown left)! Moments later, they started leaping and spinning and putting on a spectacular show! Even the tiny calves were spinning. We applauded, cheered, and thanked them. They then swam away.

High-pitched sounds

After the dolphins left, we jumped into the water and snorkeled around the reef, as we had planned to do. We were very excited to see so many colorful fish and even some sea turtles! On our way back to the kayaks, we noticed a group of pale-colored "fish" swimming far below us. As I wondered what kind of fish they were, I heard high-pitched whistling noises and knew that I was not seeing fish at all. The dolphins had returned.

We swam carefully without using our arms. We did not want to frighten the dolphins.

Surrounded by dolphins!

Glancing to my left and right, I noticed dolphins all around me and heard a noise that sounded like a woodpecker pecking. The dolphins were blasting me with **sonar**, or **echolocation** sounds (see page 27). My body felt tingly all over, and I was overcome with joy! Some people say that a dolphin's sonar can produce happy feelings in people. Perhaps my happiness was a result of the sonar, or maybe I was just thrilled to be swimming with dolphins! I swam as gently as I could without splashing or using my arms, but I did hum and sing and talk to the dolphins underwater. When I reached shore and got out of the kayak, I saw the most amazing sight! It was a wave in the shape of a dolphin!

(above) The dolphins below me looked small.
(left) This is the dolphin wave I saw at the shore. Do you think the dolphins sent it to me?

Questions about dolphins

Fish or mammals?

You know that dolphins are not fish, but how are they different from fish? Dolphins are **mammals** whose ancestors once lived on land. Fish take oxygen from water through **gills**, but dolphins breathe air above water with lungs. Dolphins are **warm-blooded** and are born live. Fish are **cold-blooded** and hatch from eggs. Fish swim by moving their tails from side to side. Dolphin tails move up and down.

how fish swim

What are dolphins?

Dolphins belong to a group of marine mammals called **cetaceans**. Cetaceans include whales, dolphins, and porpoises and are divided into two groups—*Mysticeti*, or **baleen whales**, and *Odontoceti*, or **toothed whales**. Baleen whales have comblike baleen plates in their mouths that filter food from ocean water.

how dolphins swim

Dolphins are toothed whales that have between 4 and 252 cone-shaped teeth.

What do dolphins eat?

Most dolphins eat fish and squid, but some larger dolphins prey on marine mammals. A few even eat other dolphins! Dolphins catch their food with their teeth, but they do not chew it. They swallow it whole or tear it into chunks. Dolphins get all the water they need from the food they eat, so they never have to take a drink.

Dolphins have no saliva. Their food is broken down in their stomachs.

How do dolphins breathe?

A dolphin breathes through a single blowhole that is connected to its lungs. The blowhole is not connected to its mouth or stomach, so the dolphin can swim, breathe, and eat at the same time without choking on its food. A strong muscle opens and closes the blowhole.

A dolphin must close its blowhole underwater, or it will drown.

Do dolphins sleep?

The way a dolphin sleeps has a lot to do with the way it breathes. Dolphins are **voluntary breathers**, which means they must make a conscious effort to breathe. Voluntary breathers cannot have deep sleeps. Instead, they take short naps near the surface of the ocean and slowly rise to take a breath. Scientists think that a dolphin may shut off half its brain when it rests and may keep the other half awake enough to breathe. While it sleeps, the dolphin keeps one eye open and closes the other. It also stops **vocalizing**, or making sounds.

While they sleep, dolphins stay near the surface of the water, where their blowholes are close to the air.

More dolphin facts

Can dolphins see well?

Dolphins can see well both above and below water. Strong muscles around their eyes allow dolphins to rotate their eyeballs to see ahead as well as to the sides. Dolphins also open their pupils wide underwater to let in more light and close them down to slits above water to shut out sunshine.

Do dolphins have ears?

Even though dolphins have only tiny holes for ears, they have excellent hearing both in and out of water. Most scientists believe that sound travels to the lower part of a dolphin's **rostrum**, or jaw. From there, it goes to the middle ear, the inner ear, and then to the dolphin's brain.

How do dolphins avoid predators?

Dolphins have coloring that helps them hide from predators such as sharks and large toothed whales. A dolphin's body has **countershading**, which means it is dark on top and lighter on the bottom, as shown on the left. Countershading helps **camouflage** a dolphin. If you look at a dolphin from below, its light abdomen blends in with the sunlit ocean surface. From above, its gray or black back blends in with the dark, deep waters below. Patterns on their bodies also help dolphins hide from predators or prey. When dolphins swim in groups, it is difficult to tell where one body begins and another ends.

How do dolphins find food?

Dolphins have excellent hearing and sight, but they also use another sense for finding food. All dolphins use a special system of "seeing and hearing" called sonar, or echolocation. "Echolocation" means creating sounds and using their echoes to locate prey or learn about the surroundings. A dolphin creates clicking sounds in the nasal passages below its blowhole and uses its **melon** to focus the sounds. When the clicks come into contact with prey, they bounce back, and the dolphin feels the echoes in its jaw. Its brain then interprets the echoes and creates a "sound image," which helps the dolphin "see" its prey when it cannot use its eyes to do so.

These Atlantic spotted dolphins are using echolocation to scan the sand for hidden prey.

What is a melon?

A dolphin's melon is made of a special fat and is located inside the bump on the dolphin's head. The dolphin uses its melon to direct sounds toward an object. It receives their echoes in a similar fatty deposit inside its jaw. Most of a dolphin's large brain is used to interpret the echolocation information it receives.

melon

If I were a dolphin...

If I were a dolphin...I would not have to wear a mask, snorkel, or flippers to swim. I could fill my lungs with air through my blowhole and stay underwater for up to fifteen minutes without coming up for a breath! My oily tears would keep salt water from stinging my eyes, and my flukes would help me swim fast.

If I were a dolphin...I could swim with my friends day and night. We would chase one another and make flying leaps out of the water. We could swim far away, but we would always find our families again. How could we find them in such a huge ocean? I'll never tell!

If I were a dolphin...I wouldn't need to talk on the phone. My friends would hear my whistles from far away. I wouldn't watch TV, either. I would swim around coral reefs and look at the sea turtles and colorful fish go by.

If I were a dolphin...I might belong to a school, but I wouldn't go to school! I'd learn everything I needed to know from my mother and other dolphins. I would hunt with my pod all night and play afterward with my friends. We might even toss our food in the air before we eat it, but no one would care. Dolphins don't need table manners!

If I were a dolphin...I would stay up all night and nap during the day. My dolphin body wouldn't need as much rest as my human body does, which is pulled down by gravity. Ocean water would support my weight and keep me afloat.

If I were a dolphin...I would dive deep and explore dark caves with my friends and never feel scared because I would use echolocation to lead me out of the caves again. What fun things would you do if you were a dolphin?

Learning from dolphins

What can we learn from dolphins? We can learn a lot! First we need to understand that dolphins are wild animals. We cannot judge them according to how much they are like us. We need to see them for what they are in their own world and respect their ocean home. Dolphins remind us that we, too, are part of the natural world. We need to breathe clean air, drink clean water, and eat healthy food.

Do you know that we use only 10 to 15 percent of our lung capacity when we breathe, but dolphins use more than 85 percent when they breathe? Dolphins can remind us that we need to take deeper breaths so that we can get more oxygen into our blood and organs.

Dolphins swim 75 to 100 miles a day. Do you get enough exercise? Can you walk or ride your bicycle to school?

Dolphins are social beings, just as we are. They cooperate with other dolphins to find and catch their food. Do you cooperate with your parents to help prepare your food? Do you cooperate with your teachers and classmates at school?

Many dolphins travel in mixed schools of several species of dolphins and whales. Sometimes they associate with people as well. Human beings often have a hard time accepting others who are different from them. Can you learn to think like a dolphin and accept others for who they are?

Dolphins are intelligent beings with different personalities, but they rarely have fights with other dolphins, and they don't hurt themselves. Think of ways you can avoid hurting yourself and others!

Dolphins are curious and love to investigate their world. Are you curious? Do you walk in nature and look closely at rocks, trees, flowers, and insects? Be curious—spend a dolphin day in the natural world around your home!

(above) Dolphins are affectionate. (below) In the wild, they often swim with their fins touching.

Dolphins communicate with sounds and body language. They pay attention to the slightest movements of other dolphins. A small change in the position of a flipper can signal to other dolphins where a pod is headed. Leaps can communicate the location of food. Do you communicate well? Are you aware of your body language? Do you really listen when others speak? Do you mean what you say? Do you say things to hurt others? Perhaps dolphins can teach us to become more aware of the messages we send when we communicate and to watch our body language!

(below) Why does a dolphin's smile make us feel so good? Stand in front of a mirror and observe your smile. Notice the difference between a fake smile and a real smile. How do you feel when you really smile?

Dolphins always seem to be smiling. We know that they cannot change their expressions, but we can! Can you spot a fake smile? Watch a person's eyes when he or she smiles at you. A real smile requires the muscles around your eyes to move as well. So why does a dolphin's fake smile make us feel so good? Perhaps dolphin smiles remind us of how much we love to have people smile at us. Maybe dolphins can remind us to smile more, too! Did you know that smiling can lift your spirits?

Look at these websites to find out how you can help dolphins: www.cetacea.org and www.cmc-ocean.org.

After reading this book, what have you learned about dolphins? What have you learned about yourself? How can you help dolphins in the wild? Name five ways.

"Bye for now!"

Glossary

Note: Boldfaced words that are defined in the book may not appear in the glossary

baleen whale A whale with thin, bony plates in its mouth, used to strain food from water

bow-riding Riding the current in front of a boat

camouflage Colors and patterns used by animals to blend in with their environment and to avoid predators

cetaceans A group of marine mammals, including dolphins, that have nearly hairless bodies, wide front flippers, and flat tails

charge To rush forward in a menacing way

cold-blooded Describing an animal whose body temperature varies with its surroundings

coral reef A ridge of coral in a body of water, where fish and other marine creatures swim, hide, and feed

drag The resistance caused by water to a swimmer

echolocation The production of sound waves and the reception of echoes used to locate objects and to investigate the surrounding environment

flukes The lobes at the end of a dolphin's tail

gill An organ used by fish to take oxygen from water for the purpose of breathing

instinct A pattern of behavior that is not learned but with which an animal is born

juvenile Not yet mature

mammal A warm-blooded animal that has a backbone

pod A stable unit of dolphins that live together

porpoise To leap at least partially out of water while swimming quickly

predator An animal that hunts and eats other animals in order to survive

prey An animal that is hunted and eaten by another animal

rostrum The beak-shaped end of a dolphin's head

school A large group of dolphins that may include several species

remora A fish with a suction cup that attaches itself to another fish or dolphin in order to live off its blood

sonar *See* echolocation

species Within a larger group of animals, a smaller group with similar bodies that are able to make babies together

voluntary breather An animal that must make a conscious effort to breathe

wake-riding Being pulled along in the waves behind a boat

warm-blooded Describing an animal whose body temperature does not change with its surroundings

Index

1 2 3 4 5 6 7 8 9 0 Printed in the U.S.A. 2 1 0 9 8 7 6 5 4 3